american sentencing

Jen Karetnick

This publication is a creative work protected in full by all applicable copyright laws, as well as by misappropriation, trade secret, unfair competition, and other applicable laws. No part of this book may be reproduced or transmitted in any manner without written permission from Winter Goose Publishing, except in the case of brief quotations embodied in critical articles or reviews. All rights reserved.

Winter Goose Publishing
45 Lafayette Road #114
North Hampton, NH 03862

www.wintergoosepublishing.com
Contact Information: info@wintergoosepublishing.com

American Sentencing

COPYRIGHT © 2016 by Jen Karetnick

First Edition, May 2016

Cover Design by Winter Goose Publishing
Typesetting by Odyssey Books

ISBN: 978-1-941058-46-6

Published in the United States of America

Contents

I. Epiphenomenon	1
Adult Congregate Living Facility	2
Mental Hygiene	3
Aphasia	4
Why You Can't Win Emotional Bingo	5
Bobble Headed	7
On the Way to Seder, My Husband Answers	8
American Sentencing	10
Recipe for Mithridatism	11
Migraine Chant	12
Echolalia	14
The Invention of Amniocentesis	15
Sap Burn	16
Hip	17
Self-Diagnosis: Tropical Depression	19
Walt Whitman's Boys	20
Extremities of a South Florida Mango Picker: Unfinished Sketches	21
Traction	22
Contractures: Three Clinical Patterns of Embracement	23
Epigraph	24
Milagros	25
Antepartum	26
Ode to a Lychee	28
Women on the Verge Discuss Viagra	29
Grandmother Fugue	30
At Mount Lebanon Cemetery	31

Mourning the Body	32
After Not Jogging for Three Months, Green Township, New Jersey	33
My Dear Fatigue,	34
A Moment Before Sleep	35
Husband and Dachshund, Snoring	36
Pocket Guide to the Architecture of Sleep	37
Nod	39
II. Villain Elles	40
Arrival	41
Alternative Art: The Practitioner Diagnoses My Tongue at the China Pavilion at the Miami Book Fair International	42
For Hashimoto's Thyroiditis	43
About Intolerance	44
Dirty Laundry	45
Supernumerary Nipple	46
To Menses	47
To Melasma	48
III. Monody	49
The Match	50
The 98-Year-Old Man Waits for His Blood to be Drawn at the Lab	52
Dear Stephanie	54
Night Sweats	56
Body My House	57
To a Stone, Caught in the Rube Goldberg Digestion Machine	59
ICU Prose Cento	60

Declining Anurans: Protest by Migraine	61
Dances with Pills	62
Routine for the Invisibly Ill	63
Doxie POV	65
American Dog Terrorists	66
Labor	67
Stillbirth	68
Massage Sonnet	69
Fireflies	70
View from a Revolving Door	71
Flying Vinnie	72
Warm Tuna Milkshake	76
Manufacturer Error	78
The Rules of Age	79
Memory Foam	80
Dental Epistle	82
After	83
How to Age	85
The Right to Be Forgotten	87
What My Autopsy Will Reveal	88
Will, Power	89
On the Discovery of a Mouse's Meninges Linking the Lymph to the Central Nervous System	91
Sadhu	92
Acknowledgments	93
About the Author	98
Notes	99

For those who suffer from chronic, invisible illnesses
For their physicians and caretakers
And for my brother

I. Epiphenomenon

"People assume you aren't sick
unless they see the sickness on your skin
like scars forming a map of all the ways you're
hurting."

—Emm Roy

Adult Congregate Living Facility

Peacocks nest on the roof on Nightingale Manor.
Beneath them, the inmates practice their manners—

the screamer, the barker, the wheelchaired tree
        hugger
who rolls mechanically to all manner

of reachable trunks. The barker woofs at whoever's
near, his yips and growls merely a manner

of speaking; the neighborhood dogs clear
fences to find one soul so canine-mannered,

gathering, it sounds like, at my house next door.
The screamer roars prayers with the mannered

consistency of a gas lawnmower
despite the aide's reminders to mind his manners,

and I shout, too, to any god there is for a measure
of silence to pervade my own echoing manor,

until the peacocks reproach me with tail feathers
housebroken as wood, from what I can see of their
        manner.

Mental Hygiene

I admit that my thoughts aren't as clean as they should be, spewing from my mouth with the resistance of gelatin. I admit my brain goes for days without a shower. A bath. Not even a swipe at the crevices with some Secret—

I admit that my limbic system has a little rough hide, especially on the heel. Ingrown emotions like toenails. Fungal dreams. A good periodontist might help. I mean, pedicurist—

I admit my amygdala's nut has been cracked. Invaded by clonal worms. The wooden splinter from the fishing dock my foot swallowed when I was ten. The cherry pit childhood friends said would grow in my stomach, spreading roots. To make me believe that the odor of coffee brewing is really canned tuna fish. To fool me into thinking the ring of the cell phone is an alien probe, misfiring—

I admit my hippocampus is a deep fryer for neurons, filled with rancid oil that must somewhere be dumped, that could power a car. I admit that I am frequently unfair. I admit I rarely recognize the next day what I have written. I admit I can barely remember this. Or you. Or want to—

Aphasia

When computers
become cucumbers,

take the alligator
to a brother floor.

Renew your subscriptions
for robotics. Become

an avocado for mental
health, and boldly glow

where no woman
has glowed before.

Why You Can't Win Emotional Bingo

Because in the beginning
it is a diagnosis of exclusion—

not this and not this
not this and not this

this is the first game
we will play

though I hesitate on that word
as it implies

participation
or an agreement of sorts

*

Because you can thicken
the simplest lines:

vertical for fear and rage
horizontal for self-disgust

or make it more complicated—
a finger on every other feeling

to score a pyramid or diamond
(though still no prize)

*

Because it bears repeating
that even with added features

no matter what card you draw
what you fill or don't fill in

the center position
will always be yours

and you will be playing
against yourself

Bobble Headed

Oh, waitress! I ordered
nuts but I got crazy
instead, and when I tried
to return it you were cozy
with another customer
so I consumed it anyway.
Can I speak to the manager
of this eatery? You see,
I'm allergic to my amygdala,
a pure reptilian
reaction I'm sure, a
swizzle-stick brain
response no one would pick.
Still, I'd like my money back.

On the Way to Seder, My Husband Answers

phone calls from patients, their parents or partners,
repeating what he has already said half-a-dozen times

in the office—"I know the auras are uncomfortable,
but they're better than grand mal seizures, and that's

what the meds will help to prevent"— and dispensing
predictions no one wants to hear—"No, I don't think

he'll come home; the stroke was catastrophic"—but
are asked for over and over in the hopes they will
        change,

while I shush the kids in the backseat, stop them from
        shouting
with too much apparent joy in their voices, keep the
        radio

playing Lady Gaga's "Telephone" turned down. Soon
we will dissect the Seder plate, digest the bitter

herbs, finger the salt dried on the easily torn skin
of faith. We will recite the plagues: boils, murrain,

the lice we have been visited by several times this
        year.
On this night, we will open the door for a rogue spirit

who might drink our wine but not heal vertigo; on
    this night
we will recline on a pillow that can't fuse a broken

spine. On this night, the cell phone chirps and sings,
and there are no miracles beyond what can be
    doctored.

American Sentencing

Between you and me, there is no
doubt in your mind. I have been here before
and will be again for "pseudo-
gout," "reversible lupus," diseases ephemeral as
the skeptical blink. Unimpressive, you say. It is no
difference to you. Once again, a test outcome
is negative, as if I am less than the sum of zero,
a body that registers nothing, not even the pretzel
knot of all its parts. Look down my throat. Peer
in my ears. Allow your instruments to dictate
the truth as you have learned it—
joint connecting symptoms to diagnosis,
not the tissue of intuition, not
the fatty imagination, not the instinct of the
gut that is flexible and in no way demonstrable.

Recipe for Mithridatism

Begin with a quarter teaspoon of complaint
(something small, a soupçon of joint pain,

a wink of migraine) that you can chew on
like spaghetti that is not quite cooked.

Allow the dose to increase, then salt
with symptoms to taste—a pinch of fatigue,

a dash of blurred vision, a generous dollop
of vertigo—before stirring in mother patches,

bezoars as bouquet garni, eggs that swell
and break in your armpits and neck, jaw

and groin. Invite the HHV family to dinner
(except for Epstein-Barr who drinks too much

of your good Amarone); send Hashimoto
to bed early, slicked with butter. The motor

runs, the dough thickens, and all of Pontus
will dine on fresh fare tonight.

Migraine Chant

"First I have to live inside it for an hour, two hours, half a day. If at first I said it was a room, change that to a house. But the question now is this: Is it not an entire city?"

—Tomas Tranströmer

It is an all-ages rave here
in the house of headache.

The lights are like young children
running, their bodies Morse code

in the house of headache.
Sleep is the only solution

in the house of headache,
but dreams are pigeons that peck

at the cerebral cortex for crumbs,
hidden in the pewter, ancient folds.

In the house of headache,
my left eye twitches, my left nostril

tingles, my left temple throbs,
and no politics or religion survives;

I pray only to a god that flushes.
In the house of headache,

"Traffic is unbearably slow.
The breaking news is out.

And somewhere a telephone is ringing."
In the house of headache,

there is no choice.
Soccer practice is over.

Even in the house of headache,
someone has to pick up the kids.

Echolalia

Outside, the incessant wails of peacocks,
Clever mimics of my baby's colic
Rising and rising in the humid night,
Propel me from my temporal seat.
Back arching, her legs point into pitchforks,
Stabbing my ribs as we rock and walk.
The doctor says don't over-stimulate,
Try not to bore her, burp more, medicate.
Startled, her tongue fans out to explore
Her mouth, clownish, stained with cherry-flavor
Tylenol, Orajel, Mylicon, wine
—Whatever liquid works to keep me calm—
Placebos until she wears herself out.
Only she knows what this is all about.

Only she knows what this is all about:
Placebos until she wears herself out,
Whatever liquid works to keep me calm
—Tylenol, Orajel, Mylicon, wine—
Her mouth clownish, stained with cherry flavor.
Startled, her tongue fans out to explore.
Try not to bore her, burp more, medicate.
The doctor says don't over-stimulate.
Stabbing my ribs as we rock and walk,
Back arching, her legs point into pitchforks,
Propel me from my temporal seat.
Rising and rising in the humid night,
Clever mimics of my baby's colic,
Outside, the incessant wails of peacocks.

The Invention of Amniocentesis

Mother, in your womb I am an experiment.
You pass on not immunity but its silvery underside,
give permission for the needle like an arrow to
birth holes in this temporary home, sip the fluid
like a taster of fine wines without the benefit of
a visible image. No bigger than a black widow
spider, the doctors must guess where I am,
and agree there is nothing to be done.
I am poison to both of us. Unsafe
harbor, you insist on mooring me to
your designated slip, tossed by rash after
rash of storms. I will remove myself early. Still ill,
of course you will not care for me right away. Of all the
eggs you might have nourished, I am the one who
        breaks you.

Sap Burn

It may seem like nurture at first:
Life from the hilt. Sap like silk.
But it can fail to nourish and worse,

it can scar like dried milk,
only powdered shadows to prove
it'd been there at all. Don't be bilked.

We've all been born, know the moves,
have heeled and toed the line dance
of mistakes. Nature shoves

its offspring away. Wiser to chance
the fall than stay the course.
Betrayal is worse when it comes

from the source.

Hip

I have to drag you
Id b totally kewl with it

to come away with me
if u were nicer 2 me

You keep me off-balance
Say pls sometimes like u care

like I just got off a cruise
But u always favor the other 1

I have more than just you to think about
Not like I asked 2 b born

The point is, all you do is cause me pain
Ugh do u know how hard it is

Can't you just straighten up
2 b perf all the time

instead of poking me and poking me
Y dont u just replace me, k

when if you would just make an effort
Ive got ** on speed dial

I could get on with my life
Its always abt u isn't it

Its always abt u

Its always

Self-Diagnosis: Tropical Depression

I am a fractured horizon, un-met
by either deep ocean or honest sky.
My hemmed-in thoughts melt, frown, marred by
rise, set, nova, repeat. What mullet
could leap consistently through such endless
pointillism and still know where to land?
What manatee could find space to surface,
what dolphin air to breathe? I swim with hands
ready to meet door jamb, feet to bed post.
Tentacled, toxic to all but their host,
bruises blossom like sea anemone;
sheets of silk or water draw me between.
There is little point to knowing up, down.
On days like this, it's sideways that I drown.

Walt Whitman's Boys

For Jaime Ferreyros
May your spirit always be hovering like your lens over the beach

are bathing, intermittent replicas, digging troughs with the glorious shovels of their arms. The sea has slept well in the night and allows the intrusions instead of trying to throw them out as it does when the moon is a pared fingernail, as it does when the moon is the bottom of a glass, as it does when there is no moon and the papaya trees rustle with fruit rats and wind. The water is so warm that their legs dissolve like salt tablets in the mouths of sprinters, one up to the knees, the next to the thighs, though the boys do not miss their limbs any more than the sky misses light when it is absent, and if you poured honey on them they would surely, like eels, become electric—

Extremities of a South Florida Mango Picker: Unfinished Sketches

I. Hands

are curved like shovels, fingernails of bark, alligator scales
on the epidermis of the tree, and knuckles that could be
marbles—She carries fruit the way a waitress on the last shift
delivers drinks or a mother juggles the smallest and last of her
many infants— pointed buttocks of squall-downed Irwins
nested between the splayed fingers and on her palm, sap like
urine burning her heart lines—

II. Feet

The mango picker's feet are sweat and sour, a range of auburn
saturations, flecked with leaf miners and fruit flies stuck in
spots of opossum-trumped flesh—insteps bruised from the
day's bocce of fruit—the heels an atlas of cracked cul-de-sacs
as they tramp through the grove, flip-flops squirting pits
from skins like goldfish from fists—Achilles arching under
the long pole to inch up the basket, supplicant, under so
many possible setting suns—

Traction

Abducted by surgeons, armpit opened as a clam, my elbow
hung above me like fruit for which the rest of me was a fox,
all stubborn yearning. Compelled by the mobile of flesh
and bone, I refused nurses and mothers, books and bribes,
shut my eyes to all but the pin inserted into the pockets
of my joint. Nocturnal, I barked myself hoarse: *Let go. Let
go. Let go.* Decades later I still wake up with my arm in
the air, metaphors instead of lessons learned, impatient for
liberation—

Contractures: Three Clinical Patterns of Embracement

I. Internal Shoulder Rotation (Hug)

Hold me like emotion against the muscle wall. Don't
　　　allow ease; escape.

II. Bent Elbow, Bent Wrist (Arm-in-Arm)

Flexion is more common than extension; we keep
　　　things to ourselves.

III. Clenched Fist (Hand-Holding)

Clasped tightly into the palm, fingers show us, in part,
　　　our weaknesses.

Epigraph

An offering which the king gives Osiris,
Ruler of the West, the Great God, the Lord
of Abydos. Let him give an offer-
ing . . . and he has, his torso on exhibit
in the Bass Museum, nut to a shell,
his legs lopped off and bandaged beside him
(Egyptian thrift, not Jewish custom)
in a sarcophagus first nailed for a child.
I guide fourth-graders toward the warped
and shrunken woods, Margo claiming rights:
Her mother's friend was found dismembered
on motel sheets that, sodden then dried, wrapped
her torso in plaster. The husband, Margo cites.
I pray it's the mummy she remembers.

Milagros

For example: a leg, ham-hocked at the joint,
or an arm, separated from the shoulder joint—
with prayers these cheap tin charms they anoint

courtesy of the scrap-metal vendors
who display them outside the *basilica*, vendors
who bank their pesos on spiritual wonders

that may or may not be secular in nature—
to pin these to the altar is second nature,
either that or cut off the braids they nurture

their whole lives to offer like a sacrifice
or a trade. But it's easy to sacrifice
vanity when a woman's last true artifice

is unswerving belief in a virgin birth.
Someone, somewhere, rocks with mirth.

Antepartum

The poet never or always
waxes nostalgic about motels
and lovers mismatched as sheets,
but only sometimes about
mid-range hotels like Sheratons,
the bathtubs big as barnyards
and sealed as diaphragms
where she can dehydrate herself
into an astronaut's main course
because no one waits in the next room

The poet never or always
thinks about England
where a bath is drawn
as if with a pencil and the rising
steam is that of a summer lake
on an evening damp with dusk,
but sometimes thinks
the flutter inside her belly
as she lowers into the water
is only a loon or two

The poet never or always
compares the motel room
with a car's back seat,
the lover with the one
balding at home, but sometimes

this bathtub is a coffin
and the loon a baby girl
inching away from the needle
sipping like a butterfly
from her mother's navel

The poet never or always
runs out of crème conditioner
(daily care for colored hair)
or clean towels brought by the maid,
but sometimes forgets
to wash her hair or change
the blade of her razor
and embraces instead the grimy film
and chips away at herself
with a dull or rusty tool

Ode to a Lychee

"Handsome, dense, round-topped, slow-growing," a
fine specimen of a tree, not just a tree but the keeper of
"the world's most romantic fruit," another way of saying
aphrodisiac, and it's easy to see why the translucent globe,
slick under the papery shell, yet firm, too, stretched
politically around its one, central seed (for etiquette I refrain
from "nut") appeals to the voyeur of the culinary kind, who
may dither over every element from transliteration—is it
litchi, leechee, perhaps lichee or lichi?—to aroma and taste
but must come every time to the same conclusion: *No matter
of what consequence I weigh the act, this juice I accept when I
take you in my mouth—*

Women on the Verge Discuss Viagra

Stamina. From the Latin *stamen*,
meaning thread of woven cloth. Plant parts
resemble the warp and woof, but old farts?
The boost was designed for the impotent,
not the young at heart. They can't afford
to see the blue of detached retinas
when the sky has already claimed those hues
and the days for viewing them are numbered.
How 'bout a pill to make them remember
to take out the garbage or mow the lawn?
One to defoliate the nose hairs grown?
Or better: to spark conversational vigor.
No chance of that? Then don't bring it on.
This is the last thing, the last thing we want.

Grandmother Fugue

Stranger, I cross your room
Daughter, you cross my room

looking you over as I go
overlooking me as you go—

to the window overlooking mulberries.
the window, at least, sees

Your will specifies ashes.
how my will has beat this thing to ashes.

I am never who you think I am.
I am not, you think. I am.

I wonder when I will have to arrange
So make other arrangements

chairs in the shape of a sonnet,
for this chair that shapes me like a sonnet.

hire a rabbi. It won't be long.
Hire a band. It won't be long.

The rhymes you sang to me as a child
The rhymes I sang to you as a child

I can only hum now, wordless.
I can still sing. Listen.

At Mount Lebanon Cemetery

We searched the ground for loose gravel to line
up on headstones, straightened the ivy vines
planted on the graves of my grandparents.
All four will reside here: Two on Seventh
Street, two on Mount Lebanon Avenue
in an arrangement of plots they chose to

be buried in as part of "The Socians"—the club
of Jewish men one of my grandfathers dubbed.
Wandering in herds even across seas.
We're not hard to find with trail markings like these
but we can also blend in, hard as the ground
to unearth. My other grandfather found

a brass plaque, flat in the grass, to be sufficient
—who, for God's sake, needs a monument?—
and it is this we swung aside for his wife's
burial, though it was as if she'd died thirty-five
years ago when she lost her own name, her
childrens'. Only her body we interred,
walking after a silent moment
to my parents' sites, bought midway into life.
We've gained the right to lie how we prefer.

Mourning the Body

Grieved now to think of you in silky disguise, cleats two-stepping, a misplaced Brazilian on the Jersey blades, belly to bump with a hand-sewn Diadora, indent on the forehead directing like a traffic cop, instep laces as long as night wrapped around like a gift—

Grieved to think of you in August, salt staining your cheeks, a tide come and gone and come again, calluses as big as coins, muscles itching with acid during pre-season sprints, dribbling laps, drills for foot speed, shots, passes—

You in November and the unyielding marble of thigh, taking hits like paintball shots, chilled air a snifter of liquor to the chest but still, leather smacking leather into the upper right just under the post, billowing the net—

You in the gym, Samba flats squeaking, overgrown tennis ball bouncing off bleachers, burning proof on your skin, five to a side, blizzards at a boil outside, whistles in your ears that reverb and ring—

No scars sneering on your knees, no earthquakes in your Achilles, no ache traveling from shoulder joint to elbow like a spice on the palate, that slow saffron spread—

No sunscreen, no lenses, no ball cap, no nap—

You lithe and lean, you unscathed, you unprotected, you playing, you body doing your sweet, sweet job

After Not Jogging for Three Months, Green Township, New Jersey

The pull begins deep
in the muscles the way
acid takes root in the teeth.

Stallions show me their
saffron tools as blinkered,
they trot and buck.

A caravan of Harleys
bank down the hill
I run up, most of them red

as my face, I imagine;
I can't tell if the riders
wave to me or each other

or empty flower beds,
combed like graves
for bulbs yet to be born.

A hawk paces me. I glimpse
his hunt through maples
naked as summer creeks,

lapping the stubbed cornfields.
Cold spring. Tomorrow
will bring a strain, the rub.

My Dear Fatigue,

lead me to the bed, encased
in plastic that speaks as plainly as a Saltine,

where I will dress in sticky perspiration
as if I were a mango recently broken

from its stem, the sap spurting
even as it falls from the tree. Show me

how I am incapable of being
the kind of mother who dedicates herself

to her children despite the puppetry joints,
the pebbled organs and glands the size of grapes,

the eyes that dry like laundry in the sunshine.
See me the way a lover sees another.

I admire your persistence. My desire for you
is as large or small as a dream. I know you

like a sister and fight you like a brother. Welcome,
I say, welcome. You need look no further

for a vessel to occupy, fill with your wisdom,
take your planned, unsound rest.

A Moment Before Sleep

I lower my daughter
to the mattress of her
crib as her limbs sweep
and freeze like a lobster
dropped into hot water.
A moment before sleep

she crawls from square to square
on the quilt of nightmares
and resolutions she keeps
pinned to her lids. My hair
in her fist, thumb secured,
a moment before sleep

in a formula haze
she shrieks as I release
her to rest in the deep
uncertainty of space,
to forage her own place
a moment before sleep,

and I walk as all moms
must away from the com-
fort of mutual grip,
the brisk maternal calm
an unconvincing charm
a moment before sleep.

Husband and Dachshund, Snoring

I lie bent in bed, oddly bookended
by syncopated snorts. First the inhale,
all male and busy, then the knotted thread
of well-fed breath from the female.
Oh, hale soldiers of sleep who keep my head
on the treadmill with poems—*woof*, you also smell.

Pocket Guide to the Architecture of Sleep

A reasonable person might suppose that a good night's sleep is built from the ground up, and explored from the top down. That dreams are stored in the attic, just under the barrel tiles, next to the grade school diplomas and prom gowns so pink they glow through boxes, and the deep waves (where mouths are dustpans for drool) are shelved in refinished basements with structural—not ornamental— pillars like dust-lidded jars of violet, pickled orbs, put up from the garden by old women of the ilk I have already become—

A reasonable person might suppose that a good night's sleep is earned by the body's daily destruction: staircases fumbled and door jambs misjudged, Olympic-failing floor routines in the vacuum category. Plus the amount of effort it takes—in the gym? on the tennis court?—to digest that lobster Cobb salad with poached egg and Sauvignon Blanc that tastes like a meadow of blue morning light—

A reasonable person might suppose that a good night's sleep is bought by deadlines filed, by arguments sorted and folded in the bureau drawers, by secrets swept free of the Art Deco cornices like cobwebs to catch in the blinking draft of the fan before settling to the termite-scarred Dade County pine. By the oversize French doors firmly stopped against the night and the tomcat, tired from hunting rats under the gothic-armed mango trees. By the children, freed from the

mounting ziggurat of social media, in their own rooms and
breathing evenly. The husband, in a frieze of bill receipts and
Riedel stem-less glasses—

But a reasonable person might suppose that she could be
wrong, night after night, waiting for sleep to download
from the hard drive. For renovation of the almost-image
to visitation, the remodeling of particularly troubling
nightmares. And a reasonable person could be left cooling
on the portico for so long that only cyber doorways speak
the language of design, while every poem wears the husk of a
gargoyle—

nocturnes sharpen claws
birthed in the occipital
skitter like acorns

Nod

Yes to the moth-eaten smog shimmying underneath
    the chandelier
Yes to the walls leaning Pisa-like, the stucco spitting
    paint, the baseboards shooting nails
Yes to popcorn ceilings yellowing like white pills left
    too long in a bottle on a windowsill

Yes to vertigo, nausea, acidic twisters in the gut
to kaleidoscope lamplight and halos crowding the
    corners of corneas
to voices tunneling through ears like cockroaches

Yes to hot tea in muscles, to grieving feet, to sweat as
    copious as a cat's purr and thirst as bright as
    enlightenment
Yes to the map where sex is the country of citizenship
Yes to sleep like the glaze on a doughnut

Yes to fear of elevators, fear of lightning, fear of
    flying, fear of birth
to being afraid for no reason, to no quarrel with death,
to the dream of waking soundly in the garden of
    choice, yes

II. Villain Elles

"The language of beneath the diaphragm
Has told me where it's coming from

And where I'm going, too: soft skin to rocks,
The body reveling until it wrecks . . ."

—Rafael Campo

Arrival

For Haiti, after the 2009 earthquake

Nou led, nou la. "We are ugly, but we are here,"
you say through the cracks of your lips, your hands
coated with the dust that masks any succor.

Your breasts may fall like bricks but still pucker
for the mouths of fashion-blind infants:
Nou led, nou la. "We are ugly, but we are here."

For what use, really, are French manicures,
the Lancôme creams on faces life-beaten?
Coated with the dust that masks any succor,

now and throughout the centuries, since before
the men whose blood bought freedom, those little
       Toussaints:
Nou led, nou la. "We are ugly, but we are here,"

spoken in greetings and leave-takings from mother
to daughter, cousin, friend, neighbor—women
coated with the dusk that masked any succor

until the buildings also denied their covers.
We have been fooled by muted foundations,
coated with pearlized dust that masks any succor.
Sisters, *bonjou*. We have been ugly, but we are here.

Alternative Art: The Practitioner Diagnoses My Tongue at the China Pavilion at the Miami Book Fair International

After Elizabeth Bishop

Lolling, rolling, wagging, playful—
qualities ideal for a dog;
but in a tongue? Indictful

of a pattern, the throat unable
to clear itself of growing frogs,
lolling, rolling, wagging, playful

in the ponds behind the tonsils.
And my words may have culinary swag
but on my palate? It seems indictful

of disease, imprinted like molars,
coating the surface with a fog
of lolling, rolling, wagging, playful

slime cities, the fruit of mold,
no fertile ground about which to brag.
And of such a tongue, so indictful,

there's a blue of something as yet untold
by my body's imperfect hold
(lolling, rolling, wagging, playful)
on its tongue. Well, this was (not!) insightful.

For Hashimoto's Thyroiditis

I follow idols down a scripted path
toward the reproduction of fickle cells,
swallowing substitutes like an oath.

With the return of desire is growth,
new hair, fuzzy as leaves, fingernails
punching points in the soft skin of the path,

and years released with every pent breath.
Yesterday, tomorrow, hope is a scale
that weighs substitutions like an oath,

and far above my head is the wispy wreath.
But today there is that glorious fuel
that powers me down an uncharted path,

and between day and night I can choose both;
today I dress in pearls that gleam like pills.
Wallowing in permission like an oath

I have no limits to argue with—
I can eat ice cream, pay bills, paint walls—
as long as I follow this prescripted path,
swallow forever the exact same oath.

About Intolerance

First it was dairy, then it was gluten.
These days I have no hold on anything,
my body unlike those of other women.

Eggs are my own private hurricane.
Shellfish narrows my throat to string.
Despair the dairy; give up the gluten;

these days, I can't even feast on men
without hives the size of anxiety rising.
My body unbecoming of other women,

basics for the flesh need an EpiPen
to keep the important bits from swelling.
I could drown in dairy, burst from gluten,

demonstrating: even what's healthy ends
in rupture, requires suturing.
Ban me from my own body, woman,

extract from me all the meat. But leave the bones.
They're more resilient than you think—
absent of dairy, absent of gluten,
building me into another woman.

Dirty Laundry

It huddles protectively in the bins,
hiding weeks of history, telling lies.
Do you see how it layers like intestines?

It's time to ruin a new bottle of Gain,
cover my losses with odors that please,
that fold innocuously into the bins,

permit the epic flood of evidence:
who fights; who cheats; who, at night, still pees.
Do you see how it twists like intestines?

Time again for those color separations,
clothing apartheid, delicate whites that see
Spray 'n Wash favors while still in the bins.

And time also for the cycles of pain,
the tumbling abuse of bras and panties.
See? They knot and resist like intestines,

bear stains that refuse definition,
and none of these machines offer release.
Laundry lies, in wait, in the bins.
I feel it digesting me, like intestines.

Supernumerary Nipple

This is the mistake some genes still make:
an appendix, a coccyx, an extra teat.
For this I would have burned at the stake.

Vestigial? No, I was a modern freak,
afraid to show my flat chest in a two-piece suit.
This is the mistake some genes still make—

I was told it's a freckle, a birthmark.
But with that slit nubbin, how not to suspect?
For this I would have burned at the stake,

witch and familiar in the same hot dark;
now in the fall of breast, you can't see what
a mistake the genes sometimes still make:

The third nipple, unwanted, lets down milk
while two others, regulation-size, await.
For this I should be burned at the stake

yet I put the baby's lips to where the fit is exact.
Renounce me. I forgive you. You'll forget.
This is the mistake some genes still make.
For this, I refuse to burn at the stake.

To Menses

It's not enough to say I've had it with you.
Others so afflicted feel the same:
The womb, that abacus, subtracts its due.

An unwilling accomplice, I sweat to
shoot you from the hard drive of cell and meme.
It's not enough to say I've had it with you;

pre-programmed, I can't quit until you do,
playing your eternal numbers game.
The womb, that abacus, subtracts its due,

but recall, I've contributed funds, too,
nurturing them in this bank—the very same.
It's not enough to say I've had it with you

or even fair, as there have been dividends: two
(though they have grown up to deposit blame).
The womb, that abacus, subtracts its due.

Am I really to be finished with its use,
and share no longer in this work of shame?
It's time enough to say I've had it with you.
The womb, that abacus, says my account is due.

To Melasma

I never was a pretty girl but I got by
on my legs (let's be honest), my turns of phrase,
and my skin, which had something young to say.

Now it's another sun blossoming every day.
Go ahead, disfigure me, make me so conscious
of how I can't be a pretty girl, can't get by

without cosmetics to misdirect the eye
the way metaphors conceal the same old clichés.
But so muted, I don't know what to say.

Understand, I'm not looking for advice;
I know you're immune equally to creams and pleas.
I never was a pretty girl but I got by

until this mask you left me from pregnancy
and exposure to the climate I chose.
An age spot only has so much to say.

Well, fuck it. I'll take these patches as beauty,
highlight my cheekbones with their wise shadows.
I never was a pretty girl but I got by.
And now, at least, I have something to say.

III. Monody

"How will I know
in thicket ahead
is danger or treasure
when Body my good
bright dog is dead"

—May Swenson

The Match

The young doctors herd like sheep in white
lab coats freshly bleached, clip-on photo name
tags and black felt tips lined up, the regimentals
of soldiers. Hands in well-deep pockets,
they fidget with the objects carried to test
the senses—pins, toothpicks, match-

sticks—as they mill in the auditorium to "match"
to residency programs. Framed by a white
screen, the dean painstakingly takes his annual test,
calling out, one at a time, the names
he can't see to pronounce, reading glasses in his
>pocket.
Hours earlier, the student regiment

took nine oaths, promising to "prescribe regimen
for the good of my patients" in voices that matched
each other for Hippocratic fervor, pockets
of ancient belief stitched however briefly to white-
coated supplicants, who invoked the gods by name
and prayed for no more of these awful tests

of nerves. Weren't the Board exams test
enough, those impossible blue books regimented
by medical societies with medieval names?
And the autopsies, anatomy classes that matched
students to cadavers, odors leeching faces white?
Still, some place the envelopes in their pockets

unopened, or scan the cellophane pocket
that displays only the student's name as if to further
        test
themselves, delaying the disappointment or the white-
hot flare of relief. Other members of the regiment
dip into their orders as if to a match-
less feast, shouting out the names

of their assignments, naming
the initials—ENT, OB—they'll sew onto the pockets
of their spotless coats. And then the match
is over. Four years of academic tests
behind, four of training to go, the regiment
pivots in this moment as young, white-

clad brides do from one name to another. Tests
are now for patients with deep pockets. The daily
        regimen
reassures: the toothpicks, the unlit matches. The coats
        of healthy white.

The 98-Year-Old Man Waits for His Blood to be Drawn at the Lab

He wants to fuck me!

He wants to be the big man
on campus. I've been taking that shot
for twelve years. Twelve years!

    . . . What?
I can't hear you.
I'm telling you, he wants to fuck
me. Did he even talk to the other guy?
No, he wants to be the big man.
He wants me to die like . . .

    . . . What?
I gave you the form! The card?
She has it. The wife. I don't
know where she is! She's in
cahoots with him!

    . . . He knows
nothing. That shot has been keeping
me alive, for twelve years that shot
has been keeping me alive, and he goes
and takes it away. He is a no-goodnik,
this one.

. . . Here she is! Give
the lady the card! What? The card,
the insurance, you know what card,
what, you get lost in the elevator?

. . . You two are beautiful,
you make a nice couple, just beautiful.
Stay that way, I tip my hat to you.

. . . You know, I've been taking
that shot for twelve years. He wants
me to die, he wants to be the big man
on campus. Twelve years, I need that shot,
why would I get it if I didn't need it?

. . . And here I am, I'm still here, and now
he wants to fuck me. Well, fuck him.

. . . Did you give her the card?
The insurance? Did you give it to her?

. . . Oh, you want me now?
It's my turn? You want me?

. . . You stay beautiful.

Dear Stephanie

For Stephanie Green, September 17th, 1975
-January 9th, 2011

I held your breast in my hand
the other day, the newer one,
round and hard, the size of
a mini compact disc, the one

you scanned and printed
and made into party favors,
coasters for drinks, the Old
Granddad on the rocks poured

at the corner bar, a hole
over the aureole the only nod
toward modesty, your private-
made-public joke that you handed

out at the Heeb Storytelling event.
That night, the tumors had left you
wearing the lustrous kind of wig
only Jewish girls in Miami know

where to buy, in a corset, displaying
cleavage that appeared authentic
and pearls whose aged patina
shone with promise, spinning

tales of sex and the tropics. I held
your breast and I am sorry to say
I smiled and let it sail toward the trash
despite having kept it all this time.

From another friend, who called
you "sister" on her blog, I found out
you had died, just before taking
my students to the Holocaust Memorial,

where many of them cried openly
over the photos of the nude, heavy-breasted
women forced to the gas chambers,
their heads shorn and uncovered,

while the Nazis looked on and laughed.
I said the Mourner's Kaddish for you there,
over the sculptures of Jews who had gone
from this world the way they came in,

bald, grimacing, wondering. I wish
I had held your breast, marked with
the tears of drink and condensation,
at least a little bit closer to mine.

Night Sweats

They rise upon you, flood
you in the neighborhood of sleep
where once-solid canyons of breasts,
hips, knees, parched from breath, west of age,
have slipped, begun to crack.
It's not that there's a lack of cool
breezes or even air
conditioning; matter of fact,
it's like you booked a room
in an ice hotel, framed yourself
an igloo. Still you melt,
puddle, a tongue so svelte, velvet
before fusing to steel,
teaching you reversal,
how to tread betrayal, ride luck
before lightning strikes, bringing rains.

Body My House

Eventually, the body remembers
nothing. Pierce it with needles
as if trussing a turkey; core it
like an apple for surgery. Punch it.
Kick it. Splinter its architecture
in the teeth of a wolf; burn it
with coffee poured from the wrong
side of the carafe; engulf it
with the surge of a hurricane
named after someone you know.
Organ or artery, muscle or fat,
mute and amnesiac the body
sweats it out night after night,
drenching the sheets, flushing
stalled heart rhythms, those
marshy ponds of lungs, paralytic
intestines blown up like animals
made out of balloons; the body
lets go of pain that is too painful
to recall.

      But the mind drags on
any hurt more than fist-sized
like a shadow, sometimes
eager, sometimes reluctant,
depending on the cast of light,
depending on what hour of day
or night it wishes to reexamine

its failures of composure; the mind
recalls how the shrieks of nails
torn from lumber are not at all
like the pangs of childbirth
and how unlikely is tolerance
when you most expect it; the mind
memorializes how pain rattles it,
and the ease with which its shelter
no matter how shored up
gives in.

To a Stone, Caught in the Rube Goldberg Digestion Machine

Oh, stone, I found you A) sedimentary, striated B), on a beach long ago in Boston, digging C) with other freshman; learned D) how you can be added to E) over the years but also compressed, disguised F), worn thin G) by patient effluvia; until buried H) in the peat of a human organ I), secluded in the lowest lobe J), you taught me K) body geology L), that a pebble of calculi can activate M) non-activity N) when food is raised O) to teeth and tongue P), pulling strings Q) to saliva, which initiates R), a swallow impulse S), which spills T) oxalates down a water slide U) into stomach, where it is squeezed V) into the deep pool of coils that remain W) as passive as sand, signaling X) the cessation of the self-operating Y) dignity that is easier to crack Z) than I thought.

ICU Prose Cento

Even now, when skin is not alone, it remembers being alone,
the dignity of being, alive for a short time in a very different
way, the sickly thing asserting its will only now at the end,
loitering in the morning chill, faking a French accent, the
echo calling a fossil back to name.

My horse, my hound, what will I do when you are fallen?
Chances are, the answer's missing too. The window's closed.
The wind through my heart blows all my candles out. I do
not write of riches: I have none. I am not lonely for the
palpable world. Wouldn't it be wrong not to mention joy?

With lines from poets Naomi Shihab Nye, Linda Gregg, Jennifer K. Sweeney, Dobby Gibson, Philip Levine, J. Michael Martinez, May Swenson, Marilyn Hacker, Deborah Digges, Joachim du Bellay, Reginald Shepherd and Jim Moore

Declining Anurans: Protest by Migraine

Five thousand species in the world
and tonight they are being held
in the echo chamber of my skull,
an army of amphibians culled
from swamps to make camp in my head—

Gardiner's frog of the Seychelles,
toad from Europe, fire-bellied,
frog known as American bull—
five thousand species

that screech, bark, grunt in global
tongues: the Korean *gae-gool-gae-gool*,
Russian *kva-kva*, Spanish *berp*. Hail
their loss of habitat. There's no pill
to restore one lost anuran, or refill
five thousand species.

Dances with Pills

After John Keats

You deceptive disks of false modesty,
        You Lilliputian putts down the throat,
Idle workers of mysterious ways
        To calm the limbs that club at nights in starts:
What pathways do you take, what barriers
        Penetrate, what abnormal excitements
            Do you soothe like a child at a circus?
        What quakes cease to shake? What batters to
        stir?
What nervy tantrums do you prevent?
        Or what false promises, fat
        senselessness?

Routine for the Invisibly Ill

I. Summer Version

Upon waking, it's time to take my pills.
But first, I pick from my lashes the pills

of cat hair and cosmetics I've failed to wash
down the mouth of the drain like pills;

I pee and read *People* in which people like me
and also not like me complain about their pills;

I walk the dogs and collect dozens of mangos,
those overgrown, puckering pills;

try to persuade my husband it's his turn
to filter water and grind French-roasted pills;

I drive my kids to soccer camp so they can kick
into nets and heads the bloated pills

that give them aches and pains in closed-up places
like stubborn, blistered packets of pills;

throw into the dishwasher a few plates
and powdered detergent compressed into pills;

head to my office to answer the phone to listen
to the automated message informing me that my pills

are ready to be picked up, start the computer
and stare at the words staring back at me: black, bitter
      pills.

II. Winter Version

It is not Alice who grows but the pills
I swallow like foul language, pills

half as big as the size of my thumb,
capsules I could open into a drink (pills

filled with poison) when someone's
back is turned. Nor is there a pill

of hope that I can ever stop washing down
not just meds but these oblong and opaque pills—

vitamins, antioxidants, supplements—
that accumulate on my chart like pills

on a sweater. It's as if I wear my cells
outside in, or my skin with holes, pills

pricked into its whole so miniscule they can't
be seen but also can't be sewn, pills

that let everything valuable escape, pills
for which there are no plug-shaped pills.

Doxie POV

After Theodore Roethke

The medicine on your breath
could make a small dog dizzy;
but a partner in all things death,
I vowed to make this easy.

You placed me carefully
between rib and hip like a shelf.
We slept until the days
could not preserve themselves.

The sweat that drenched my fur
I licked for its pickling salt.
Your heart raced like Ben Hur.
Your dreams I absorbed by default.

You hauled yourself from bed
in dust-drenched afternoons
to return with fistfuls of bread
and the promise of less to come, soon.

American Dog Terrorists

Blood is what they want so it's blood
they'll get. Crawling from shrubs they'll
sabotage the host, sabotage
being their first nature, being
not animals, not humans, not
insects but spiders, ticks in sects,
eggs carried like ideas, eggs
the seeds of disease, unnoticed the
way they attach, feed, make headway
in reorganizing origin.

Labor

In the womb of the furnace
the glass can only imagine itself.
Sibling between sand and lava,
it is a nova on the end of my pole
that I must power like a spit
so that it doesn't fall slow-motion
in a luminescent globule on my foot
or worse, the floor. Dip into tint
and spin; wash in water and spin;
return to flames and spin as cramps
sweat under my skin and I unlock
the damper of my diaphragm, loosen
and harden in turn to breathe, breathe,
breathe this body into being.

Stillbirth

For Noam, and Adam

Outside he could only imagine his worth.
Never before did he have to be still,
gathered, sunken, for the weight of work,
the allowance of sound, and light's strange pull.

Never before did he have to be still,
the spacious brine permitting leaps and dives,
allowing rough sound and light's strange pull
to be kept, always, at a wall's remove.

The spacious brine permitting leaps and dives—
when did that all seep so quickly away?
Having been kept, always, at a remove,
her pulse was a river he felt to see.

How did it all seep so quickly away?
He was ready, they said, for the weight of work.
But his pulse was a river that failed to be.
Outside, we can only conceive his worth.

Massage Sonnet

At Mandara Spa, Aruba Marriott, remembering Deborah Digges

Offer yourself in the way of a child,
splayed and unconcerned about the curl
of a limb, the arrangement of towel
revealing the shell of shy genital.
The hands that wave and recede deal with parts,
oiling rusty mechanisms. Submit.
Allow your mouth to drool. Show all your warts.
This is the hour your best poems will visit,
and your worst. Later, you can only rescue
so many words but some will be enough
to compensate for this half-conscious theft.
Do only what you have been told to do:
Relax your arm; roll over; focus your breath.
So much, or so little, time might be left.

Fireflies

Under the hurricane lantern of a hornet's nest,
insects blinking in and out to smooth the mud
as if with cat's tongue or potter's hands, bugs
in the dark blue space between oak branches and
        grass
pulse and burn the way of a migraine, light up
like questions that have no answers or would have
no answers if anyone thought to ask them,
brief as the air in the jar of childhood Augusts,
Morse code for the females who wait in the gloom
to mate them or to eat them, depending on
their staccato moods, beating throughout the night
like my father's heart in the emergency room,
seized by glass eyes under machines and by grid,
collective breath held tight that might loosen the lid.

View from a Revolving Door

Outside the ER I watch two cats mate,
stacked like wood in the fire lane, silent,
the subject not open to the usual debate.
Inside, no ill appears emergent.
The only wails are those from a child; spit
bubbles from her mouth as she tries to break
free of her papa's lap. Just another shift
at Palmetto—the uninsured here for check-
ups, flu shots, drug refills. Most wait still
as wax plants. He'll be discharged at nine
though he'd been admitted for the night, ankle
pinned ahead of time. I freeze with the felines
as automatic doors swing like clock hands.
Either way it's crutches—one lover, one friend.

Flying Vinnie

After a sculpture by Dan Daniels

He's refused a drink from flight attendants,
not because the absence of absinthe
or, hollow as pipes, he is made from the lint
of rust. His iron was formed to stand
in gardens with others of his sort who
tip their hats to rain and hail from the straws
poking out from the undignified maws
of paper drink cups filled with slushy hues
never seen in nature, though likely viewed
through the fae eyes of life on an easel.
Simply, he is more taken with the field
of clouds ungluing next to his windowed
seat, and complains about my decisions:
Lack of canvas will cost him his visions.

Lack of canvas will cost him his visions,
though his arm is forever raised with brush
at the ready, poised to jab as if to box,
and he whines to anyone who listens—
a toddler kicking his seat from behind,
the elderly woman on the way
down the aisle who calls me Dorothy,
businessman, soldier, selfie-taking student
with her finger in the metallic wound

of his mutilated ear. "Wet Willie/Dry
Vinnie," she captions on social media,
going viral as soon as we land.
No *thank you* for purchasing him a seat
instead of sending him wrapped in a crate.

Instead of sending him wrapped in a crate
in the frozen digestion of the plane
like a dog or stowaway immigrant,
bundled in plastic so bubble-bright
it's more luminescence than protection,
I piggy-backed him as in my youth
I did my own son, surprised by such depth
for someone so incomplete. "Woman,"
Vinnie said from behind my ear, "you hold
me too close to the bristles. Ease up the grip.
Try for a sensitive, painterly tip."
I didn't tell him only one painting sold
before his suicide, that his weight is
now of a coffin, his mien of a terrorist.

Now a coffin, his mien a terrorist—
it hurts us not at all at security.
Though a sculpture, he's still a celebrity,
an apparent, un-humbled anachronist.
It was the easel that caused the problem.
Welded to his right foot, rising upright,
it didn't fit with him in the flight's
limited overhead compartment.
In the end, I was forced to amputate
his vocation, mark it with my address

American Sentencing 73

and send it to wait with the confused mess
of last on and first off: strollers, car seats,
and walkers. Then I bought him an extra
ticket in the exit row for the room,
tried not to think about bank account gloom.

Trying not to think about bank account gloom,
I ask Vinnie, "Why all the sunflowers?"
He snorts. "I've heard people say they were
painted by me for Paul Gauguin's room.
That *pisvlek*! He was the worst houseguest.
I regret inviting him to Arles.
He didn't even come to the hospital."
This wasn't the incident with his chest
when he put a bullet into it instead
of painting landscapes of the Auver fields
but the one with a razor where he yielded
a lobe rather than whiskers from his head.
He says something about "*la tristesse*."
He says, "I wish I could pass away like this."

He says, "I wish I could pass away like this."
"You did," I tell him. "You died in the arms
of your brother, leaking your scarlet charms.
Fading to yellow, you were dismissed."
He says, "Speak to me not like a poet
for the good of all; no one reveres such
garbled intent. Express yourself as much
as you can your kernels of content."
Will a snack soothe him? Probably not.
Nervous as he is, were he born this era,

he'd be lactose intolerant, gluten-free,
deathly allergic to all kinds of nuts.
Not responsible for his temperament,
still, I am sorry for this circling current.

I am sorry for this circling current,
but growing so tired of his sadness,
his melancholy for Yellow House,
lectures on Japanese woodblock prints,
his memories of the brothel woman
to whom he gifted his ear—what a choice
that proved to be, his act spreading like a rash
over a town crying for his commitment.
Perhaps I should have overlooked his bulk
at the gallery among the daintier,
bent-steel figures of Toussaint and Renoir.
Now against the glares of others, I block
Vinnie's access with Jet Blue blankets
and request a drink from the flight attendants.

Warm Tuna Milkshake

The Aussies sit on the slippery-dip
and laugh, watching Ilene wind
as if she were a timekeeper
the piece of playground equipment
no one has a name for and only
Mal has a reason to ride
when she dares him with her ladder
of a smile. This is after he sings
to her in the laundry but before
she joins him on the top bunk
in the dormitory attic they share
with three others the night they smoke
the good black hash he smuggled
in his sock from Amsterdam,
and as he kneels on the rusty
platform, allowing himself to be
twirled, she asks him to think
of a warm tuna milkshake, testing
his strength of stomach, spinning him
faster and faster, waiting for his first
admission of weakness from the psychedelic
whirl of jungle gym, fence, and sidewalk
poodles, and when he finally shields
his eyes from the sight she jumps
aboard, risking ankles and Yankees
baseball cap to kiss him hard
on the forehead the way a Viking

in search of adventure planted
his feet in the soil of his ship,
or a gypsy about to marry
embarked on a carousel, already
moving clockwise.

Manufacturer Error

What can you do
when someone says,
"I can't fix you?"
You are the complex toy
that came minus parts,
the build-it-yourself-
with-no-instruction-chart
plywood bookshelf.
Still, the technical faults
and their ragged seizures,
jerry-rigged for few jolts,
play in the key of minor.
So you collapse occasionally.
You weren't his to fix anyway.

The Rules of Age

Last three months or seventy-five years,
with various later surprise attempts,
photograph the quiver of errors
spread before you, witnesses
lit like cigarettes in the libraries.
Don't apologize. A heart is too
often contrite. You can't run downstairs,
recreate that wild turmoil, those few
bitter passions. Bring up a chair to thinning
hair, eyeglasses—your manner a telegram
to an egghead who explodes into thinking.
Before meeting Mr. Chairman, there's time
only to nod at material fruits
before they become your neat gray suits.

Memory Foam

remembers all the cats that have slept
on your head, threading their claws with
your hair, already too thin,
kneading the reducing
dough of you, your neck
like a drill bit
(turn, turn, turn);
recalls
sweat—

and cosmetics you never wash off
because lifting water to face
even as early as dusk
is effort that could cost
you the whole next day;
memory foam
remembers
migraine
nights—

absorbing the heart palpitations
like miniature lawnmowers,
the legs that jerk, kick, and squirm,
electrified muscles
that send the wrong
messages
to your
brain—

but a mattress and pillows can't fight
the foul breath of flat disbelief,
won't offer more orgasms
or take you to dinner,
and memory foam
lies like lovers
who promise
chicken
soup—

yet pour you wine, resist the body's
nightmares that begin with falling
and end with paralysis;
it has limitations,
only gives back what
it gets from you,
whether it's
purrs or
moans—

Dental Epistle

Dear Molar #15,

My grief over losing you is no doubt disproportionate.
I should move on through the denial, the anger at that
mechanic of the mouth who lit the slow-burning candle of
anesthesia and cracked you open like an engine. I should get
on with the bargaining
of brush, polish, and floss that can never bring you back,
reassure the rest, "Don't worry
about me"—

A mother with children to spare or sacrifice, I have so many
more just like you: dedicated, hard-working, a team player
though worn to the bone. They need attention, too—

Still, those you've left behind do not have the same precious
metal, my sweet, my darling
tooth, cradler of gobstoppers and gummi bears, snapper of
chewing gum, dependable cracker of sunflower seeds and
beer bottle caps, the last to grow in, yet the first spoiled rebel
to speak up—

After

*For Amy and Eric Gardner, in honor of Jeffrey
Gardner, September 11, 2001*

Dreams of a body, a body of dreams.
On the sea's surface, a slick of weeds.
This day has no history in its seams.
This day is a garden of unfurled seeds.

On the sea's surface, a slick of weeds.
The summer's stories were of sharks, attacks.
This day is a garden of unfurled seeds.
Autumn blazes early with browns and blacks.

The summer's stories were of sharks, attacks.
Swimmers shed limbs as if to mark where they've
 been.
Autumn blazes early with browns and blacks.
In your dream, he is once again whole and clean.

Swimmers shed limbs as if to mark where they've
 been.
He smiles at you, leaning on a fence.
In your dream, he is once again whole and clean.
For brief seconds it almost makes sense.

He smiles at you, leaning on a fence.
This day has no history in its seams.
For brief seconds it almost makes sense.
Dreams of a body. A body of dreams.

How to Age

Expect that when lying down,
the breasts will take cover
in armpits; this is common

even among the barely budded.
But also know that someday
cheeks will sag towards ears

and the folds of your neck
will meet at the spine like old
friends at Starbucks, lingering

over pumpkin spice lattes,
and the creases you discover
mapping your chest in the mornings

no longer plump themselves
during the day's hydration
but instead offer directions

to mortality. Thoughts, too,
slide sideways, wrinkle
like poorly packed button-downs

on a vacation out to sea. Ignore
platitudes. You will never again
look good for your age; age

is not just a number; age isn't
only in your head, a mindset
of possibilities and limitations.

Certainly you will consider
how and what to fix, dress
too young, drink too much

before coming to terms with
the bandwidth of each exhausting
decade. Make sure to read

the fine print. There are no returns,
not for money back or store credit,
not even for merchandise in kind.

The Right to Be Forgotten

But is that really the question?
Or is it about the right to be deleted?
In Europe, the judges say yes: Request
your own kind death, manage your legacy,
negotiate terms foreign to perception, that larger

court of public opinion. But strained through
the grill of Google like plankton, digested
in the stomach of an indifferent internet,
won't even a sense memory be left, an identifying
brand in the top of the palate, residue lodged

like nut particles between the cracks
of the teeth, criticism like indigestion surfacing
without warning from the esophagus
of hardware? You may choose not to look
but the family Bible has become public,

every deed on display, missteps and triumphs
captured alike in bytes. This is where you can
create yourself but also can't erase yourself,
and where you will live on, image orbiting out
of control long after your accounts have been closed.

What My Autopsy Will Reveal

The glass houses of organs were bottles
with ships atilt inside. Stones made fences
where not even dust should have been raised.

Hits were recorded, not recovered from; meals
became anthropologic; wisdom was lost
long before memory was impacted like molars.

A tree damaged more than fifty percent in a storm,
this body, split along the sap lines, should have
long ago been removed, stump dug up,

trunk ground down, its remains spread
over the mango roots to fertilize the living fruit,
the one task it could embrace without failure.

Will, Power

Being of brain fog and broken body,
I leave to no one specific
and none intended
the white spaces that used to be words

and the streets I once recognized
and still drive, fire hydrants and curbs
leaping in front of the hood and under
bald, mismatched tires

I leave the bones that ring
like an untended alarm
and the joints that grind, gears
in the hands of a teenage driver,

leave the nerves, inflamed,
that prickle bottoms of feet,
the lymph nodes as big as
tropical fruit and egos,

my vision that changes
acuity on a blink,
a beach for the tide of white-
capped degeneration,

my tonsils that blister,
my nostrils that blister,

my cervix that blisters and
my mind that wanders, blistered

I leave lactose intolerance,
gluten sensitivity, egg allergy,
the inability to digest fruit,
the gut twisting like appetites,

the stomach dammed
and overflowing. I leave
the night sweats that salt
sleep with fevers and chills,

I leave the dark geometry
of eyes and cheekbones
in the eternal dusk of fatigue,
I leave the lack of athletic sex

I leave a governor's pardon
for my natural killer cells,
disorganized, defeated,
deserting the front lines

I leave pills downed by the fistful
I leave heralded quick fixes
I leave the unmade bed, unfluffed pillows
I leave no more witnesses

On the Discovery of a Mouse's Meninges Linking the Lymph to the Central Nervous System

The cerulean pills below my eyes
can be neither absorbed nor disguised,
multiplying like a computer worm

down the angular screen of my cheeks,
jaundiced by decades of doctors
and denial and the theory of the blood-

brain barrier. But when you mine for diamonds
with the right machinery at the correct geo-cache,
the nodes of this flat, infertile plane might yield

at least the coal that could fuel the cold oven
of survival, and my exposed ribs expand
like a bellows whose breath is held and held,

a lady in waiting eager to warm a palm, cool
a brow, or flick an eyelash from a fingertip
in order to make one last, outlandish wish.

Sadhu

If you make yourself
a ghost with the snow
melt from mountains,
the ash of brief,
ascetic fires, you were.
You are. You will be
in a hut in a village,
a temple in the city.
In the cave of perpetual
pilgrimage, it matters only that
rebirth is a truth
everyone else has missed.

Acknowledgments

Adirondack Review, "Stillbirth"

Alimentum Journal, "About Intolerance" (print only) and "Ode to a Lychee"

Autumn Sky, "Walt Whitman's Boys"

Based, "Mourning the Body"

Black Cat Lit, "Traction"

Black River Review, "At Mount Lebanon Cemetery" (the second part of "In Two Movements")

Blue Unicorn, "Sap Burn"

The Boiler Journal, "Sadhu"

CHEST, "American Sentencing"

Cleaver Magazine, "Night Sweats"

december, "Recipe for Mithridatism"

Digital Americana, Part I of "Routine for the Invisibly Ill" (formerly titled "Daily Pills, Summer Version") and "Will, Power"

Drexel Online Journal, "Nod"

Ekphrastic, "Flying Vinnie"

Folly, "Echolalia"

The Gambler, "Bobble Headed"

Gravel Magazine, "Hip"

The Healing Muse, "On the Way to Seder, My Husband"

Hospital Drive, "Dear Stephanie" and "Pocket Guide to the Architecture of Sleep"

The Intima: A Journal of Narrative Medicine, "Aphasia" and "Dances with Pills"

Isotope: Journal of Nature and Science, "Adult Congregate Living Facility"

JMWW, "ICU Prose Cento" and "Massage Sonnet"

Journal of New Jersey Poets, "After Not Jogging for Three Months, Green Township, New Jersey"

Mount Hope, "Labor" and "What My Autopsy Will Reveal"

The New Poet, "To a Stone, Caught in the Rube Goldberg Digestion Machine"

Poetry Midwest, "Milagros"

Poet's Market 2013, "Arrival: A Love Villanelle for Haiti"

PulitzerRemix.com, "The Rules of Age"

Quail Bell Magazine, "Contractures: Three Clinical Patterns of Embracement"

River King Poetry Supplement, "Epigraph"

River Styx, "A Moment Before Sleep," "Grandmother Fugue," and "The Match"

SLAB, "Memory Foam"

Sou'wester, "Antepartum"

Snapdragon: A Journal of Art & Healing, "About Intolerance" (digital only)

The Spoon River Poetry Review, "Warm Tuna Milkshake"

Stickman Review, "Fireflies"

Sweet, "Migraine Chant"

Tigertail, A South Florida Poetry Annual, "After"

"Body My House" is included in the anthology *The Burden of Light: Poems on Illness and Loss*, released in March 2014.

"Doxie POV," "Extremities of a South Florida Mango Picker: Unfinished Sketches," "Husband and Dachshund, Snoring," and "The Rules of Age" appeared in the 2015 Warnborough College Conference of the Arts anthology.

"Dirty Laundry," "Supernumerary Nipple," "To Menses," and "To Melasma" were finalists in the 2010 Knightsville awards and published in *The New Guard* under the title "Villain Elles."

"Dear Stephanie," "Massage Sonnet," and "On the Way to Seder" were finalists in the University of New Orleans Study-Abroad Prize.

"Night Sweats" placed second in the Southern Writers Symposium Competition for poetry.
"After" has been made into illuminated art and hangs on the wall of the B Bar in The Betsy Hotel, South Beach.

"The Invention of Amniocentesis," "Women on the Verge Discuss Viagra," and "On the Way to Seder, My Husband" were featured in the Saturday Poetry Series on www.howitoughtobe.com, edited by Sivan Rotholz-Teitelman.

Many thanks to The Betsy Hotel, South Beach, and its philanthropic program for a residency in summer, 2012, during which some of these poems were completed.

This manuscript was a semi-finalist in the Trio House Press competition. Some of these poems first appeared in the chapbooks *Necessary Salt* (Pudding House Publications, 2007); *Bud Break at Mango House* (Portlandia Press, 2008, winner of the Portlandia Poetry Chapbook Prize); *Landscaping for Wildlife* (Big Wonderful Press, 2012); and *Prayer of Confession* (Finishing Line Press, 2014).

About the Author

Jen Karetnick is a poet, an author, and an educator who has had published works including the poetry collection *Brie Season*, and the award-winning cookbook *Mango*. Many of her poems, stories, and articles have appeared in such publications as *Cimarron Review*, *Poets & Writers*, *Miami Herald*, and *USA Today*. Jen works as a creative writing director at Miami Arts Charter School, and the dining critic for *MIAMI Magazine*. She lives with her husband and two teenagers in Miami with their three dogs, three cats, and fourteen mango trees.

Notes

In "Recipe for Mithridatism," the word mithridatism refers to the condition of immunity acquired by taking gradually increased doses of something. It was coined after Mithridates VI, the king of Pontus, who tried to build immunity against poisoning.

"Migraine Chant" was inspired by and uses the title phrase of Tomas Tranströmer's poem, "The House of Headache," published in *The New Yorker.*

"Walt Whitman's Boys" was written ekphrastically to an iPhone photograph taken by artist Jaime Ferreyros.

In "Epigraph," the quote with which the poem begins was taken from a prayer on a mummy' casket on display at the Bass Museum of Art, Miami Beach.

In "Ode to a Lychee," the quotes come from various encyclopedia definitions of lychee.

In "Pocket Guide to the Architecture of Sleep," the title is cribbed from a book, *Pocket Guide to Miami Architecture*, which I discovered in the Writer's Room during a residency at The Betsy South Beach, Miami Beach.

The title of "Body My House" comes from a May Swenson poem.

"ICU Prose Cento" uses lines from poems written by the following poets: Naomi Shihab Nye, Linda Gregg, Jennifer K. Sweeney, Dobby Gibson, Philip Levine, J. Michael Martinez, May Swenson, Marilyn Hacker, Deborah Digges, Joachim du Bellay, Reginald Shepherd and Jim Moore.

"Labor" was written after a visit to the Glassblower's Workshop, Steninge Slott, Sweden.

"Flying Vinnie" is based on Dan Daniels's life-size sculpture of Vincent Van Gogh at an easel, which is owned by my parents.

"The Rules of Age" is found poem using words and phrases in the Pulitzer Prize-winning book, *Advise and Consent*, by Allen Drury, and were written as part of the 2013 National Poetry Month initiative sponsored by *The Found Poetry Review* and the journal's editor-in-chief, Jenni B. Baker.

"On the Discovery of a Mouse's Meninges Linking the Lymph to the Central Nervous System" is written for Antoine Louveau, the University of Virginia post-doctoral researcher who found the vessels that connect the lymphatic system to the brain in 2015. Formerly, physicians believed the lymphatic system stopped before the brain. The finding is considered so important that medical textbooks need to be rewritten.

www.ingramcontent.com/pod-product-compliance
Lightning Source LLC
Chambersburg PA
CBHW051347040426
42453CB00007B/450